Table of Contents

INTRODUCTION

A nonprofit organization (NPO) is a business that has been granted tax-exempt status by the US Internal Revenue Service (IRS) on the basis that it advances a social cause benefiting the public in some way. (Think: historical preservation, scientific research, animal welfare, economic development.) These entities are not permitted to distribute profit toward anyone or anything other than advancing the organization.

Nonprofits are sometimes referred to as non-stock corporations, or 501(c) (3) organizations—depending on the subsection of the tax code's Section 501 that provides for their tax-free status. While enjoying federal tax benefits on income, nonprofits typically must pay employment taxes for hired staff. Individual states may offer even more tax benefits to nonprofit organizations, such as exemption from paying sales taxes on items they purchase for use by the business.

Nonprofits run with the purpose of maximizing revenues for the causes they support—a key point of distinction from other types of tax-exempt organizations, which may not necessarily run with the goal of generating revenues but simply maintaining an ability to pay overhead. Virtually all charitable organizations carry a non-profit status.

A nonprofit organization (NPO) is one that is not driven by

profit but by dedication to a given cause that is the target of all income beyond what it takes to run the organization.

Because of this, NPOs receive tax-exempt status from the federal government, meaning they don't have to pay income tax.

Nonprofit organizations are often used for trusts, cooperatives, advocacy, charity, environmental and religious groups. Many, but not all, NPOs have paid staff in management positions; almost all use volunteers.

Unlike for-profit businesses, NPOs have no owners and any surplus profits after operating expenses are used to further its goals instead of being distributed between members or employees of the organization.

DIFFERENCE BETWEEN AN NPO AND A NOT-FOR-PROFIT ORGANIZATION

Nonprofit and not-for-profit are both widely used to refer to NPOs but there are subtle differences.

The United States Internal Revenue Service (IRS), for example, uses not-for-profit to refer to activities like hobbies in which revenues are not involved.

What is the difference between an NPO and NGO?

The terms NPO and NGO (non-governmental organization) are also often used interchangeably but they have some key differences.

NGOs are separate from the government and require no government council but depend on the government for funding by means of government grants.

However, most NGOs are also nonprofit organizations and thus have nonprofit status.

How does an organization qualify for NPO status?

For a nonprofit corporation to qualify as a government-recognized and tax-exempt organization, it has to fulfill conditions set out by the internal revenue code. In the United States, the IRS determines the validity and tax status of NPOs.

These qualifications include the following:

- The organization must be created for religious, charitable, scientific, literary or educational purposes.
- The organization cannot be created for the benefit of any individual or private interests.
- The organization must have a governing body that is democratically elected.
- The organization must have bylaws in place that state its purpose and how it will be run.

Organizations that wish to be granted tax exemption must attest to these conditions and file the proper paperwork with the IRS.

What are some common use cases for NPOs?

There are many use cases for nonprofit organizations. Some examples include the following:

- advocacy organizations campaigning for public safety, social welfare, political change or some other social cause;
- charitable organizations working to alleviate poverty or provide relief in times of natural disasters;
- educational institutions such as schools and

universities;
- environmental groups working to protect the planet and its resources; and
- religious organizations dedicated to spreading their faith.

Some of the more recognizable types of nonprofit organizations include the American Red Cross, Amnesty International and the United Way.

What Is The Difference Between "Public Charities" and "Foundations"?

501(c)(3) organizations are divided into two main categories, "public charities" and "private foundations." Public charities are 501(c)(3) organizations that get their support from the general public, government. Donations made to public charities are usually tax-deductible. Private foundations conversely distribute money via grants to fulfill a public purpose. Contributions to private foundations are normally tax-deductible. Private foundations are also not allowed to engage in direct lobbying activities.

KEY DIFFERENCES BETWEEN NONPROFIT AND FOR-PROFIT ORGANIZATIONS

Purpose

All companies have a distinct purpose, but this is where the difference between a nonprofit and a for-profit is the starkest. While for-profit organizations may have a variety of goals, their primary mission is to generate profit and develop effective products and services that are valuable to consumers. Companies develop products and services that either directly solve a problem or increase overall efficiencies, such as the case with mobile phones or autonomous vehicles. A nonprofit, by contrast, doesn't prioritize profits and is instead dedicated to promoting a social cause or advocating for a particular standpoint. Examples of nonprofit services often include assisting with basic human and environmental needs such as food, water, education, endangered species, forests and wildlife. These services strive to solve important, potentially life-threatening problems and issues. Therefore, success for nonprofits is measured based on an organization accomplishing its philanthropic mission.

Funding

One of the most important aspects of running an organization is establishing a consistent method for funding projects and operations. For-profit organizations tend to fund their initial efforts through bank loans, local investors and revenue generated from sales. If a company's product or service is considered to have a high potential market value, then they may have the opportunity to receive funding from national or global investors, such as angle investors and venture capitalists. Nonprofits often take a different approach by seeking out private donations of time and money, corporate sponsorships, and government grants, among others. Crowdfunding, a form of online fundraising, has also become a popular method of funding for nonprofit organizations as of late.

Diversity of Audience

For-profit companies can have a much more defined target audience than that of a nonprofit. In a for-profit, the company seeks to reach and establish a relationship with consumers who will purchase their products/services to help generate revenue. This relationship creates a continual feedback loop, allowing the company to increase its revenue and expand its offerings to reach new target audiences. Rather than delivering a product or service directly, nonprofits are typically approaching their audiences with a message about a product, service or action. Nonprofits must reach a more diverse audience which can include volunteers, donors, corporate sponsors, and the general public. Due to this broad audience, nonprofits must carefully consider the interests of each segment of their audience.

Leadership

The executive leadership of a for-profit company is typically quite clear. Whether it's a privately held small-business or a large corporation with boards and stakeholders, leadership responsibilities are distributed amongst a select group of individuals. These individuals are considered not only leaders, but also have a stake in the financial success of the organization, which often results in incentives such as bonuses and profit sharing. Due to this, for-profit leaders are primarily concerned with profit and increasing revenue for the organization. By contrast, nonprofit organizations tend to be led and directed by a board of directors who guide the future of the organization without possessing direct financial ownership. The board can be anywhere from 25-30 members to upwards of 100 members. While not concerned as much with financial success, the leadership does have to balance financial concerns alongside social and/or environmental issues. In this case, leadership meeting agendas tend to include a wide array of topics such as funding for upcoming projects, social climate, environmental concerns, organizational performance, fundraising, social and political policies, and potential community concerns that need assistance or funding.

Organizational Culture

The differences in a mission can lead for-profit and nonprofit organizations to establish two distinctly different organizational cultures. Due to the goal of financial gain, the culture within for-profit organizations tends to focus on finances and business metrics, such as key performance indicators (KPIs). Employees are also encouraged to be innovative with the creation of new products and markets, all of which can help increase short- and long-term revenue for the company. The culture within a nonprofit is often more community-oriented, as employees are often asked to address and solve problems that have little financial incentive (ex. advocating against deforestation). With this community-oriented culture, it's common to see employees of non-profit organizations advocating for the organization outside their work schedule. This could be attending an evening fundraising event or handing out educational resources to local businesses on the weekend.

Taxation

Typically, nonprofits are registered as a 501(c)3 organization, which means that they are able to provide their services as a public good without rendering a portion of their earnings back to the government. Likewise, individuals and companies donating to these organizations are able to write off their contributions as tax-deductible. For-profit companies are not able to benefit from tax exemptions and must pay taxes as the law requires.

Staff

The workforce of a nonprofit can be wholly different than that of a for-profit corporation. While a for-profit corporation will consist mostly of paid employees and interns, a nonprofit typically relies heavily on volunteer staff. This element links up with many other aspects of a nonprofit company, as these volunteers will also frequently be on the front line representing the nonprofit organization's mission to potential future donors.

BENEFITS OF A NONPROFIT ORGANIZATION

Not all civic, social sports or other organizations that aren't money motivated need to formally become nonprofits. While starting a nonprofit organization can be a big undertaking that requires extensive planning, financing and the support of a dedicated team, in some cases, it's a relatively simple task.

Nonprofits range from organizations that provide health, arts, environmental, advocacy, civic, cultural or human services. Although each nonprofit is different, nonprofit benefits are consistent from one type to another.

Easy and Inexpensive to Start

You can start a nonprofit organization by visiting your secretary of state's website and filling out some simple paperwork. The application fee is usually less than $100. If you want to become a federally tax-exempt organization, that will take more paperwork and money.

Access to Grants

Similar to starting a for-profit business, starting a large nonprofit requires funds to pay for leasing or purchasing office space, buying equipment, hiring a staff and for programming. Nonprofits have a wide variety of financial resources available to them, beyond loans. They have access to various grant programs designed to help them fund their organizations, explains Candid Learning.com. In many instances, the grants available to nonprofit businesses differ from what's available to for-profit businesses. Access to grants is one of the key nonprofit organization benefits.

Reduces Your Liability

Even though nonprofits don't seek profit, they are still set up as legal entities. Unlike a sole proprietorship, nonprofit organizations function as limited liability organizations, points out FindLaw.com. This is advantageous for owners because it keeps their personal assets separate than what happens with the nonprofit organization. For example, if an individual sues the nonprofit, limited liability prevents a suit from also being filed against the owner.

Tax-Exempt Status

Non profits can file for 501(c)(3) status and become eligible as tax-exempt entities. Qualifying organizations, such as schools and churches, are exempt from paying local, state and federal taxes. Their exempt status helps keep more money in the organization for events, activities, equipment and supplies.

Tax-Deductible Contributions

Companies and individuals who donate to nonprofit organizations who have 501 (c)(3) status can write their contributions off during the tax season. Nonprofits can highlight this benefit in their fundraising materials to help persuade people to donate to the cause the organization supports.

If companies arrange for sponsorships with nonprofits, they can often deduct this expenses as a marketing cost, which means you don't need to go beyond becoming a nonprofit at the state level (i.e. obtain 501(c) status) to attract sponsors.

Pursue Your Passion

Individuals often form nonprofit organizations to fulfill a passion they have; whether they lost a family member to a disease, were in an abusive relationship, want to mentor young kids or want to spread awareness about environment concerns. As a nonprofit owner you get to realize your passion, while sharing it with others who hold a similar interest.

Positive Community Involvement

Nonprofit organizations are set up to provide services that benefit communities by providing resources and support. From art centers, which teach children how to draw and make creations using pottery, to organizations designed to help entrepreneurs launch their businesses, each nonprofit contributes to the overall growth of its community.The Different Types of Nonprofit Organizations In The United States

Technically under the IRS's 501(c) code, there are two main types of nonprofits: nonprofit organization (NPO) and not-for-profit organization (NFPO). NPO's serve the public via goods and services while a not-for-profit organization (NFPO) may serve just a group of members. 501(c)(3), are organizations that are "corporations, funds or foundations that operate for religious, charitable, scientific, literary or educational purposes." Conversely, NFPOs may exist for more private focused groups or members. Other types include:

- Section 501(c)(4): civic leagues and social welfare organizations, homeowners associations, and volunteer fire companies.
- Section 501(c)(5): such as labor unions
- Section 501(c)(6): such as chambers of commerce.
- Section 501(c)(7): such as Social and Recreational Clubs
- Section 501(k): childcare-related organizations.

There are also others. The U.S. Internal Revenue Code contains many different classifications of tax-exempt groups.

REASONS WHY YOU SHOULD START A NONPROFIT ORGANIZATION

When you think of a nonprofit organization, you might immediately call to mind large charities such as the American Cancer Society, the ASPCA, or religious societies. Nonprofits exist in almost every sector: education, health, law, politics, art, and sports. Even companies such as Meta and Tesla have extensive nonprofit arms.

A nonprofit doesn't have to be a large charity. It can be more like a small club to support individuals in a community, or even an educational arm to complement your business.

According to the National Council of Nonprofits, 92% of nonprofits have annual revenues of under $1 million. Think of booster clubs, financial aid groups, and even your local PTA – all small but necessary nonprofit organizations.

Here are the top reasons why you should start a nonprofit organization:

You likely have limited liability

If your nonprofit is designated as a 501(c)(3) and in compliance, your organization's founders and employees are protected from legal action. This means that you are not personally responsible for any debts incurred by the nonprofit, nor are your trustees or employees.

You can spin off a nonprofit from your business

Do you focus on education as part of your business? Or do you regularly meet with groups who could use some support? Form a nonprofit for this area and take advantage of the benefits of nonprofits while maintaining your regular business.

Your business will enjoy greater market visibility and penetration, as it sponsors the nonprofit. You can also attract funding from large companies or foundations that treat companies with nonprofit arms more favorably.

You are eligible for financial benefits

Many business suppliers, landlords, and service providers offer discounts or sponsorship to nonprofits. Services such as e-mail marketing may be provided free of charge.

In addition, nonprofits can be eligible for federal and state grants that for-profits cannot use. You can use these grants, which do not have to be repaid, to fund overhead and operating costs besides the charitable service. Nationwide, almost 32% of nonprofits' revenue comes from federal grants.

You can register as a tax-exempt organization

This gives you special tax status under federal law. You can collect tax-deductible contributions, be exempt from federal unemployment tax, and even enjoy reduced postage rates.

The IRS maintains a page for tax-exempt organizations, with webinars, FAQs, and informational pages.

You can increase your business' visibility

People are likely to pay more attention to a business with a non-profit arm. They see it as more trustworthy and more honest.

Nonprofits often make the news when they sponsor a new initiative or law, open a center or other building, or have a fundraising drive. You have a chance to create donors from customers and vice versa.

You can help drive the economy

Nonprofits' payrolls are greater than most other industries, including construction, transportation, and finance. The nonprofit sector employs over 12 million people.

This has a knock-on effect – nonprofits themselves employ people. The people they serve may be able to rejoin the economy and contribute to their own and their community's well-being financially.

You can gain leadership and organizational skills

Many business leaders got their start working at nonprofits. Nonprofit entrepreneurs are also famous in their own right as successful leaders, social advocates, and savvy businessmen and businesswomen.

You can take charge of issues close to your heart

Creating a nonprofit enables you to support a cause you care about in a greater way than with an individual donation. The same business skills and tactics used in for-profits apply to nonprofits.

You don't have to know all the details of establishing a non-profit, as long as you have the drive and desire. Many organizations will walk you through the steps in creating a nonprofit, offering resources to help you concentrate on your vision.

You can create a legacy

Being involved in a nonprofit shows other businesses, financiers, and the public that you care about a social issue, not just the bottom line. You are improving the economy along with making a real difference in people's lives.

In addition, you have the satisfaction of creating something greater than yourself that will evolve to have a life of its own because of your efforts. One of the oldest nonprofits in the US was started in 1636 – Harvard University!

When you consider the financial, economic, and social benefits of starting a nonprofit, you can see why there are over 1.2 million of them in the US alone. Add your strengths in business to the nonprofit sector, and leave your stamp on the future.

THE BENEFITS & DISADVANTAGES OF FORMING A NONPROFIT COMPANY

Do you have as a goal addressing a societal problem? Or maybe forming a social club, trade organization, or cooperative? If so you may be wondering if you should operate informally or if your goals could best be accomplished by incorporating.

If you are looking to earn a profit as well as accomplish those other goals, then you would want to form a for-profit corporation, LLC, or benefit corporation. But if you are not looking for profit then you should consider the benefits of forming a nonprofit company. Most nonprofits are formed to provide a benefit to the public, as opposed to clubs, cooperatives, etc. that are formed to benefit their members. They include companies formed for charitable, educational, scientific, religious and literary purposes. These charitable companies are also referred to as Sec. 501(c)(3) organizations, after the section of the Internal

Revenue Code that provides them with an exemption from taxation.

Below are some of the benefits of forming a statutory nonprofit company (usually a corporation although an LLC can be a nonprofit as well), rather than continuing to pursue a nonprofit purpose as an informal group or association.

Benefits of forming a nonprofit corporation

Separate entity status

A nonprofit corporation (or LLC) has its own separate existence. It can enter into its own contracts, sue and be sued in its own name and is responsible for its own contractual and other obligations. In an informal or non-statutory nonprofit, the person entering into contracts in his or her own name can be liable if there is a breach of the contract.

Perpetual existence

A nonprofit corporation or LLC has a statutory right to exist in perpetuity. An informal organization does not have that.

Limited liability protection

A nonprofit corporation (or LLC) protects directors, officers and members (if it has any members) against being held personally responsible for their company's debts and liabilities. Because that limited liability protection is provided for by statute, an informal organization does not have that.

Tax-exempt status

Nonprofit corporations (or LLCs) can apply for both federal

and state tax-exempt status. While a group or association that has not been formed under state law can apply for tax-exempt status it is generally easier for a statutory business entity (and especially a corporation) to get IRS approval.

Access to grants

Some nonprofits are eligible to receive public and private grants, making it easier to get operating capital. For instance, certain grants and other public allocations are only available to 501(c)(3) organizations. Tax-deductible donations. With 501(c)(3) nonprofits, donations made by individuals to the nonprofit corporation are tax-deductible. Possible state sales and property taxes exemption. This benefit varies by state but nonprofit companies may be exempt from paying sales and/or property taxes.

US Postal Service discounts

Tax-exempt nonprofits generally can receive discounts on bulk mail rates.

Credibility

There may be more established credibility for a nonprofit corporation than for a person or persons informally trying to accomplish their nonprofit purpose. Donors may prefer to donate to nonprofit corporations because of this credibility.

Professional registered agent

Statutory nonprofits like corporations and LLCs have to appoint a registered agent. This gives them the ability to appoint a professional registered agent, which helps ensure proper treatment of the critical, time-sensitive court documents that will be served in the event the nonprofit is sued.

Disadvantages of forming a nonprofit corporation

Below are some of the disadvantages of forming a statutory nonprofit corporation (or LLC).

Expenses

Forming a statutory nonprofit company requires filing documents with the state business entity filing office - which means filing fees. In most states there will be annual fees to pay to the state as well. And although a professional registered agent is recommended, there is a cost for that too.

Ongoing compliance obligations

Statutory nonprofits also have to comply with the provisions of the statute under which they were formed. That can mean, among other things, the need to file an annual report, draft bylaws (or an operating agreement), retain certain books and records, and make filings with the state upon certain important changes to the company.

Management oversight

Nonprofit statutes – especially nonprofit corporation laws - closely regulate how the nonprofit is to be managed. For example, the law may require a board of directors, periodic meetings, quorums, minutes, and other compliance obligations to which informal nonprofits are not subject.

No lobbying or political campaigning

Tax-exempt nonprofits have restrictions on their lobbying and political activities, which can affect their ability to advocate for their causes.

CHECKLIST FOR STARTING A NONPROFIT ORGANIZATION

Starting a nonprofit can feel like entering a new world with a completely different language at times. Trying to keep track of all the steps you need to accomplish can quickly become overwhelming.

Setting up a new nonprofit organization requires a lot of different steps, and you want to be sure you don't miss anything within the process.

Creating a nonprofit can be a complicated process, so a checklist can help you and everyone on your team stay on track and on the same page.

A checklist can also help minimize the chances of becoming overwhelmed, and can make the steps seem more attainable. An organized checklist can help you clearly see your path to a new organization.

Simplifying the process into these key steps will allow you to maintain clarity within your nonprofit, which will build trust among the community you serve and donors you invite to join your mission. Each step within this checklist will take intentional thought and time, but it will be worth it in the end!

DEFINE MISSION, VISION, AND VALUES

The first step when starting a nonprofit is to define your organization's mission, vision, and values.

You may inherently know these things as you think of the nonprofit work you want to begin, but it deserves time and energy to develop statements that speak to funders who may not be as close to the cause as you are.

So what's the secret to creating a powerful mission and vision statement? Take a few hours with those working alongside you, or alone, and brainstorm keywords that capture the essential reason why your nonprofit exists. Ask yourselves:

- What would happen if we did not exist?
- If we are successful in every way, what will change?
- What are the 1-2 things that would make our existence matter?

If you can answer these questions clearly, you can write powerful statements, drawing funders in who will be just as passionate about the work as you are!

Once your mission and vision are crafted, think of the values that will drive your organization from start to finish. These will guide everything from your programs and staff to your volunteers, board members, and donors.

Values should not be static words. They should be core ideals that guide the work being done each day through the work of your nonprofit organization.

DO RESEARCH OF THE SPACE AND AVAILABLE GRANTS

All nonprofits require funding to exist. Research the types of grant funding that are available for the services your nonprofit will provide.

See what other nonprofits exist that might be serving your same mission. See what type of funding they have received, and make note of certain funders who may share your passions as you begin your new nonprofit organization.

You can also use databases that list funders, their areas of interest, and all available grants to understand the landscape of funding available to you. You want to be sure that the mission you are seeking to carry out has a need in your community and has potential funders to back it.

If you do not see funders that align with your mission, vision, and goals, you may want to go back to the drawing board. Consider programs you could add that might align with the needs of your community and funder's passions, or consider adding your work in collaboration with another organization that is closely related.

CHOOSE A NAME

Here's the deal: There are millions of nonprofit organizations. You want to choose a name for your nonprofit that grabs your audience's attention and easily explains the work you do.

The worst thing you can do is have an organization name that confuses funders. Find something meaningful that people can identify and relate to from the start.

ESTABLISH YOUR NONPROFIT TEAM

Any good business takes a team of support to be successful. Nonprofits are no different. Whether you have funding for staff or if you are an all-volunteer team, here are a few tips for establishing your team:

- Create an organizational chart
- Define team roles
- Develop a workplan
- Utilize volunteer committees

If your nonprofit is a solo effort for now, that's okay. You can still build a team to help you accomplish everything on your starting a nonprofit organization checklist. Find one to two people in your circle of influence that have skills to contribute. Whether they have a creative mind to help you bounce ideas off of, or if they are an organizational guru, let them lend their skills to help you accomplish your goals.

BUILD A BOARD OF DIRECTORS

Every 501c3 nonprofit organization is legally required to have a board of directors. What does that mean for you? Part of starting a nonprofit organization includes finding the right people to serve on your board of directors. If you don't yet have a team of volunteers helping you, reach out to your community.

Find your local United Way, a local community foundation, or a nearby university. These institutions are often key stakeholders within the community and might know individuals who want to serve nonprofit organizations.

Board members should bring needed skills and a passion for your work. As you bring in individuals to serve as board members, you will want to give them clear direction.

Consider drafting board member job descriptions. These descriptions will help them know exactly what to expect as they consider joining your nonprofit organization.

LEGALLY INCORPORATE YOUR NONPROFIT

To gain funding from private donors, foundations, and grants, you must legally incorporate your nonprofit. This can be the most cumbersome part of starting a nonprofit organization, but that's the beauty of a checklist. Follow each step, mark your progress, and you can finish strong!

While every state has specific requirements for incorporating your nonprofit, here are a few basic steps required nationally:

- Complete your Articles of Incorporation and file them
- Draft bylaws
- Hold an official meeting
- Apply for a Federal Employer Identification Number
- Apply for federal tax exemption
- Familiarize yourself with initial state requirements
- Register as a charity

It is extremely important to keep records of everything within this process. Funders will often ask for documentation that you will receive through the process above with each grant application. Save your files as a PDF so you can easily upload or share them upon request.

BUILD AN ONLINE PRESENCE FOR YOUR NONPROFIT

One thing that must be on your starting a nonprofit organization checklist is building an online presence.

Many funders will get their first impression of your organization online. Three places you should focus on are your website, Guidestar profile, and social media.

Website: the goal of your website should be to clearly explain your nonprofit's purpose and build trust with donors.

Use images and bold fonts to clearly highlight your mission, vision, and programs. When funders land on your website, these are some of the first things they should see.

List your staff and board of directors. Even if you are volunteer-led, list the people who are leading the organization. Use a headshot and list their profession. This is an easy way to build confidence and draw in funders.

Make your Donate Page clear and easy to read. Always include your physical mailing address for those who want to mail a check. Include your EIN, as many foundations will pull this information when considering you for funding.

Social Media Platforms: Decide which social media platforms make sense for your organization to use and create business profiles. Start off with small goals:

- Post at least once per month on each platform
- Share your mission and vision to orient new donors to who you are

Share stories of success about:

- Your programs
- People you are serving
- New board leadership
- New funding received
- Partnerships in the communities you serve

Start small and grow your online presence to help develop credibility behind your organization.

START APPLYING FOR GRANTS

By now, you should be ready to start securing funding. The next step is to apply for grants!

You will find that the amount of information on potential grants is abundant. Rather than trying to create your own way of gathering, storing, and remembering all of the different funders and areas of interest, utilize a system that makes it easy for you.

Using this system, you can gather the opportunities that you have a high likelihood of receiving funding from.

Ask yourself:

- Which ones do you fit best with their funding areas?
- Which ones are you eligible for?
- Who has open opportunities?

One helpful tip is to create a skeleton grant application, gathering the main items you will need for any application:

- History about your nonprofit
- Mission and vision
- List of board of directors
- Program descriptions and expected results
- Organizational budget

- 501c3 letter

You can tailor these items to fit the requirements for different grant opportunities. Having these items in one place will allow you to more quickly complete grant proposals and secure funding.

NONPROFIT BOARD MEMBER RESPONSIBILITIES

It is essential for all nonprofits to have a strong organizational infrastructure, including an effective Board of Directors. In fact, the Board of Directors is a key component of any nonprofit's success.

A Board of Directors is the governing body of a nonprofit organization. Nonprofit board responsibilities include providing oversight and governance to the organization. Board members typically serve for a specific length of time, called a term, which is outlined in the nonprofit's bylaws.

A Board of Directors has several different positions, including a Board President/Chair, a Vice-Chair, a Treasurer, and, often, a Secretary.

While board members are typically volunteers, their responsibilities are significant.

It's impossible to do a job well if you don't know what the job is. A Board of Directors is no different! All board members must take the time to understand their roles and responsibilities, starting with these fundamental legal obligations:

- Duty of Care: Each board member is responsible for making decisions on behalf of the organization they are serving and exercising their best judgment in doing so.
- Duty of Loyalty: Each board member must put the organization's interests before their own personal and/or professional interests.
- Duty of Obedience: Board members are legally responsible for ensuring the organization complies with all applicable federal, state, and local laws and adheres to its mission.

But this is just the beginning! In addition to the three core legal responsibilities, nonprofit board members have a number of other responsibilities as well.

DETERMINE THE ORGANIZATION'S MISSION AND PURPOSE

It is the board's responsibility to create and uphold the nonprofit's mission statement and purpose, which should articulate the goals and desired impact of the nonprofit and the constituents served. This should take the form of a written mission statement that is widely distributed to staff, board members, community members, and other key stakeholders.

The mission statement should explain what makes the nonprofit unique, clearly express the organization's goals, and make a compelling case for why individuals, corporations, and foundations should financially support the nonprofit.

In addition to ensuring the mission statement exists, the board should periodically review the statement's adequacy and accuracy.

SELECT THE CHIEF EXECUTIVE

Hiring and overseeing the work of the nonprofit's CEO/Executive Director is one of the most important responsibilities of a board member as it significantly impacts the organization's performance, growth, and sustainability. The executive director or CEO also serves as the liaison between the Board of Directors and the organization's staff.

The responsibility of hiring and selecting the chief executive may fall to a select few board members or a designated hiring committee, depending on the organization's size.

Sometimes, when a nonprofit's chief executive departs the organization, the board will engage with an organizational consulting firm to conduct an organizational assessment. This assessment analyzes the organization's strengths and weaknesses and provides information to the Board of Directors to inform the selection and hiring process.

The board also plays a key role in determining appropriate compensation for the organization's chief executive. It is important for nonprofit organizations to ensure that their salaries, even those of the highest-ranking officials in the organization, are on par with other nonprofits of their size and scope to comply with IRS regulations for tax-exempt organizations.

SET COMPENSATION LEVELS

An organization's Board of Directors is also responsible for establishing compensation policies and guidelines. This is important for nonprofits because the IRS limits nonprofit salaries to "reasonable compensation," meaning nonprofits can face penalties, such as fines, for overpaying their staff and/or executives.

Board members must ensure that consistent guidelines are documented to determine salaries for the organization. This doesn't mean that the Board of Directors needs to agree on the salary for every individual employee; rather, boards should agree on salary ranges for each position that their organization has and allow the appropriate staff (executive, HR director, etc.) to determine the salary for all staff members.

MAINTAIN FINANCIAL INTEGRITY

One of the foremost nonprofit board responsibilities is to preserve the organization's financial standing. Board members serve as trustees of the organization's assets, meaning they are responsible for ensuring that the nonprofit's financial status is healthy. Some of the primary financial responsibilities of board members are:

Budgeting: Board members, in collaboration with the CEO/Executive Director, set the organization's budget each year. A specific committee, such as a Finance Committee, may be charged with compiling the budget in larger nonprofits.

In smaller nonprofits, the Board's Treasurer may work one-on-one with the executive to set the budget. Regardless of who compiles the annual budget, it should be formally approved and adopted by the full Board of Directors each year.

Accounting/Reporting: The board is responsible for ensuring proper accounting and financial reporting is happening at all times. Nonprofit organizations must legally account for all income and expenditures with appropriate bookkeeping practices and report on their financials via Form 990 each year.

Some states may require state-level reporting as well. It is the board's responsibility to ensure that these functions are occurring and that they are being done properly.

Investment Oversight: Not all nonprofits have investments; however, many do. These investments could be things like property, stocks, or an endowment. For those that do have investments, the board plays a critical role. A documented, board-approved investment policy should outline how the organization will invest funds in a responsible, ethical manner.

This is especially important because the IRS requires nonprofits to satisfy the "Prudent Investor Rule" in relation to any investments, which requires a fiduciary to invest the organization's assets as if they were their own, and prohibits overly risky investments.

SUPPORT FUNDRAISING EFFORTS & PROTECT RESOURCES

Similar to the financial and fiduciary responsibilities, board members must also ensure that a nonprofit organization has all the resources it needs to succeed and be sustainable. What does this look like?

Board members should be involved in fundraising efforts in some capacity each year. Many organizations write this responsibility in their bylaws or board member job descriptions to ensure that the expectations are clearly documented.

Achieving 100% board giving is important for all nonprofit organizations as it shows potential funders that the entire board is engaged with and supportive of the organization.

ADHERE TO LEGAL RESPONSIBILITIES

Every Board of Directors must understand the organization's internal policies and procedures and the legal implications of the organization's operations. Board members must understand relevant federal, state, and local laws that apply to the nonprofit and ensure that the organization adheres to those regulations.

For example, all tax-related filings must be done correctly and on time, including state and federal tax returns. Nonprofits registered as 501(c)(3) organizations are exempt from income tax but must still pay payroll and property taxes. Failure to file the 990 form with the IRS can result in the loss of tax-exempt status.

There are other offenses that could result in penalties that board members should be aware of, such as overpaying staff or contractors and engaging in excessive lobbying or political activities.

ENSURE EFFECTIVE ORGANIZATIONAL PLANNING

The Board is responsible for short- and long-term strategic planning. These efforts should be made in collaboration with the organization's executive team, the full staff, and other important stakeholders.

The board should work collaboratively to make realistic plans that honor the organization's mission and vision and consider the needs of the constituency the organization serves.

The most common type of organizational planning a nonprofit undergoes is the strategic planning process, a long-term planning document that outlines strategies that will enable the nonprofit to meet its goals.

RECRUIT NEW BOARD MEMBERS & ASSESS BOARD PERFORMANCE

The board is also responsible for recruiting new board members in partnership with the nonprofit's chief executive. Once new members are identified and recruited, board members are responsible for orienting the new members.

Periodically, the board should conduct a self-assessment to evaluate their performance and identify areas in which the board may be able to be more effective.

ADVANCE THE NONPROFIT'S MISSION

A nonprofit's board members are its most important advocates, serving as the 'face' of the organization and vocal supporters of its cause. Board members should leverage their skill sets and personal and professional networks to promote the organization's mission, programs, and services to the public.

Because a nonprofit's board of directors will likely have diverse and varying skills, this may look different for each member. Some board members will have connections to potential big donors or some might have connections to the media to generate free PR content.

The important thing is that each board member identifies ways they can support the nonprofit by tapping into the people they know and the skills they have.

MONITOR THE ORGANIZATION'S PROGRAMS, SERVICES, AND PERFORMANCE

The board sets the mission and vision of the nonprofit, and as such, they play a role in ensuring that the organization's programs and services stay true to that mission.

Board members should have detailed knowledge of the programs and services offered by the organization, who participates in those programs, and the outcomes and impact of them.

This ongoing monitoring helps the board accomplish other key responsibilities, such as short and long-term planning and financial oversight. If the board is not aware of the organization's programming and impact, they will not be able to execute these key tasks.

SUPPORT & EVALUATE THE CHIEF EXECUTIVE

In addition to hiring the chief executive and determining fair compensation, the board is also responsible for providing an annual performance evaluation to the Executive Director/CEO.

The board should create a clear, documented process for the executive's evaluation and identify specific board members to carry out this task on behalf of the entire board.

NONPROFIT BYLAWS

Nonprofit Bylaws are a legal document that outlines how an organization will be governed. Bylaws manage the membership requirements, frequency of meetings, amendment procedures, voting procedures, and more.

Bylaws are considered the operating manual for a nonprofit organization. They consist of:

- Duties and roles of officers and directors
- Rules regarding how the board of directors will function and its size limit
- Rules regarding the procedures for electing directors, holding meetings, and appointing officers
- How the funds received from grants will be distributed
- A description of the conflict of interest procedures and policies
- Other relevant corporate governance issues

Nonprofit governance issues will usually be addressed by state nonprofit law. The bylaws of the organization may be customized based on the nonprofit's requirements, as long as they don't violate state law.

The bylaws of a nonprofit are not filed publicly, but they do add transparency and accountability to the actions taken by the officers and board of directors. The bylaws should be updated and amended as the organization evolves and grows. Under the Internal Revenue Code (IRC) Section 501(c)(3), a nonprofit organization is required to file an annual return and must list any changes to the name, address, and structure. For example, an annual report should notify the IRS of any changes made to the bylaws that occurred during the course of the year.

The Exempt Organizations Determinations Office should be notified of any changes to the bylaws if the organization isn't required to file an annual return. Remember, there are some states that will require nonprofits to file and report changes made to the bylaws. A nonprofit's bylaws may also be referred to as a:

- Nonprofit corporation bylaws
- Bylaws for nonprofit organization

HOW TO WRITE YOUR NONPROFIT BYLAWS

When writing a nonprofit's bylaws it's important to remember that there's a difference between the words "shall" and "may." "Shall" is generally used to express an intended provision in the form of offers or suggestions. On the other hand, "may" is generally used to express possibility or permission. Also, check the laws in the state in which the organization has been incorporated to make sure the bylaws meet state requirements.

Your local Secretary of State office should be able to supply the applicable laws for your nonprofit. The bylaws of a nonprofit organization will typically contain the following 12 articles:

- Name of the organization: The name of the nonprofit organization
- Corporation purpose: The purpose of the nonprofit organization
- Membership: Define who is currently a member and how an individual becomes a member
- Meetings of members: Address when the meetings of the members will occur
- Board of directors: Identify the general powers,

tenure, requirements, and qualifications of the board of directors

- Officers: Outline what positions will be created for the executive officers
- Committees: Illustrate what and how committee will be formed
- Corporate staff: Express the intent of the nonprofit to hire corporate staff
- Conflict of interest and compensation: Describe how to protect the nonprofit when entering into a transaction that potentially benefits a member of the board of directors or an officer
- Indemnification: An indemnification clause is added to the bylaws to help prevent employees and board members from being sued
- Books and records: Define where the complete book and record of bylaws will be filed
- Amendments: Explain how the bylaws may be amended

NONPROFIT BYLAWS – THE DO'S AND DON'TS

Do: Get help in creating and amending the bylaws from expert. A professional services firm or an attorney may be able to add some assistance. Two things to take into consideration:

Don't assume your current attorney understands nonprofits

Bylaws are a legal document and the board of directors should supply input and vote to adopt them

Do: Be as simple and basic as possible. Stick to the addressing the highest levels of governing issues, such as:

- Board structure
- Organization purpose
- Officer position responsibilities
- Meeting requirements
- Voting rights

Do: Follow-through with the intentions of the bylaws

Do: Hold the board members legally responsible for understanding and adopting the bylaws

Do: Keep the bylaws relevant

Don't: Get so detailed that the bylaws turn into a corporate procedure and policy manual

Don't: Include bylaws that restrict future boards from acting effectively or efficiently

Don't: Forget to review the bylaws on an annual basis

HOW ARE BYLAWS USED

Bylaws are used to guide the board's actions and decisions. They are helpful in preventing or resolving conflict and disagreements. They can protect the organization from potential problems by clearly outlining rules around authority levels, rights, and expectations.

How Are Nonprofit Bylaws Created and Amended?

The board creates bylaws when the organization is established. Don't operate without them. States have different statutes that apply to bylaws — some dictate specific provisions, while others give more general guidelines. Find the state regulations from your Secretary of State's office or your state attorney general's office. If your organization operates in more than one state, follow the laws in the state where the organization is incorporated. Once created, an attorney can review them to ensure they meet the legal requirements of the state.

Bylaws are not static, and the board should review them regularly. They should accurately reflect how the organization works and remain relevant, and this requires amending the bylaws periodically. Keeping bylaws simple in language and content can help ease this process. Some organizations appoint a task force to review and make suggestions for revision, reporting findings to the whole board. If the board votes to amend the bylaws, mark the revisions on the bylaws and record the date that they were amended, and r. Report any major structural or authority changes in your next Form 990.

What Should You Include?

Bylaws are individual to an organization, but they should cover certain issues:

- Name and location of organization
- Statement of purpose
- Election, roles, and terms of board members and officers
- Membership issues (categories, responsibilities)
- Meeting guidelines (frequency, quorum)
- Board structure (size and standing committees, if any)
- Compensation and indemnification of board members
- Role of chief executive
- Amendment of bylaws
- Dissolution of the organization

HIERARCHY OF LAWS

While bylaws are a detailed and immediate source of regulations, they must follow federal and state laws and comply with your organization's articles of incorporation. If there is a contradiction between the bylaws and these other regulations, that part of the bylaws is invalid. For bylaws to be concise, the board also should create comprehensive policies and resolutions.

What if Bylaws Are Ignored or Broken?

There may be several reasons why an organization does not follow the bylaws, and there are different ways to address this. In some situations, bylaws are ignored because they are no longer relevant to the organization. Either they are too broad, have not been revised for several years, or are not in practical or understandable language. If this is true, the board should make revision a priority.

Both board members and others involved with an organization should be concerned when bylaws are intentionally broken or not amended. There are a few avenues of recourse in this situation.

Internal

If you are a board member, inform the board of your concern, and make sure your objections are noted in the minutes. As the bylaws are a legal document, similar to a contract, there can be legal repercussions if they are ignored; therefore, it is important for the board to take any concerns seriously. If you are not on the board, share your concerns with the board chair or chief executive, or, if the board holds public meetings, address your concerns there.

Chamber of Commerce or Better Business Bureau

You can file a complaint with these organizations. These groups cannot enforce the bylaws, but they do keep records of complaints, and their public nature will give exposure to the issue. This may get other people involved who can encourage the board to comply.

Court

The bylaws are a legal document, so there is a possibility for prosecution if they are intentionally broken. This is a long and expensive process, and often the courts are reluctant to get involved in internal organization issues. Going to court may also jeopardize the future of the organization as a whole.

State attorney general

This office has authority over all nonprofits, and it can require the organization to change its bylaws, comply with the original bylaws, or force the organization to close. Like the courts, however, state attorney generals are reluctant to get involved in internal organizational issues.

Organizations thrive when they have the right policies and structures in place to support their success, and the guidance of nonprofit bylaws are an integral part of this. Whether you are learning to build bylaws for the first time or reviewing what you have instated, your board can best protect your organization and create greater cohesion within your nonprofit by prioritizing, updating, and adhering to your bylaws.

NONPROFIT BYLAWS BEST PRACTICES

There are a few best practices to keep in mind when developing your nonprofit bylaws. These will ensure your bylaws are accurate, transparent, and remain current.

Get professional help

As flattering as it is to have you reading this article to begin your journey toward creating your nonprofit's bylaws, please don't mistake this piece for legal advice. Nonprofit bylaws are legally binding and a board can be held liable for breaching them. Therefore, it's best practice to seek professional legal advice when forming yours.

If you're lucky, you might have a lawyer on your board of directors who can help you parse out all the subtle nuances between using "shall" versus "may" versus "must" versus "can." There may also be low-cost or pro-bono lawyers in your area who can walk you through your state's not for profit corporation law, and answer any questions you might have around how your responsibilities differ from an S corporation.

State laws can dictate some of the details of your bylaws, such as the minimum number of board members you're required to maintain. Rather than feel overwhelmed trying to make sure you've met all legal responsibilities pertaining to your bylaws, invest in professional help.

Include only your basic foundations for governance

Since nonprofit bylaws are legally binding, they should include only the fundamentals for your operation, like how frequently your board will meet and how membership will make decisions. You want to avoid including anything that is likely to change frequently, such as how many fundraisers you'll hold each year or exact titles for staff positions you'll hire.

Also, lean toward being general over specific. For example, rather than say your board will meet every second Tuesday of each month at 5:30 p.m. in the main conference room located at 555 Nonprofit Way, just say your board will meet monthly. Keeping bylaws general allows for needed flexibility in scheduling and strategic planning.

Include topics that regularly change and other nuanced details in your organizational policies rather than your nonprofit bylaws.

Be transparent about your bylaws

Build trust with your supporters by being transparent about your bylaws. The public should have easy access to your bylaws to help hold your nonprofit accountable in its operations. You can house them on your website, and may even consider announcing them on your nonprofit social media as you kick off your incorporation. Strong bylaws establish your nonprofit brand as one donors can trust with their money.

Conduct periodic reviews for any needed updates

Even though bylaws include only the basics of how your nonprofit operates, they may still need adjustments over the years as your nonprofit scales. Plan to review your bylaws as a board around every two years to see if you should vote on any amendments.

ARTICLES OF INCORPORATION

The articles of incorporation are the papers submitted to the government for the legal formation of an organization. The process of drafting, submitting, and getting it approved by the state is known as incorporation.

The articles of incorporation are the foremost requirement for forming an NGO and are submitted to the secretary of state to register your organization in the state's record. Since all NPOs apply for tax exemption, the IRS also requires it to prove your nonprofit status.

Each country has its guidelines and fee for creating the articles of incorporation. Depending on the state, the filing fee in the US ranges from $100 to $250. In some states, the articles of incorporation are also known as 501c3 articles of incorporation, certificates of formation, or even charter documents.

Are Articles of Incorporation and Bylaws the Same Thing?

The articles of incorporation are often confused with another legal document, "by-law" but there is a significant difference between them.

The 501c3 articles of incorporation describe the purpose of your NPO, while a by-law describes how your nonprofit will carry out its day-to-day operations.

They also differ greatly in terms of their contents. The corporate charter contains detailed information about an organization and its members, such as name, address, mission, directors, and registered agent. On the other hand, bylaws define guidelines to manage their operations such as recruiting team members, selecting board members, and initiating new projects.

Why Are the Articles of Incorporation Important for Nonprofits?

The articles of incorporation 501c3 are the primary document required to form your NPO. They register you with the government, explain the purpose of your organization, and determine your board of directors.

The IRS only approves your tax exemption if your articles of incorporation are approved by the federal state. Therefore, they are the foremost requirement for seeking tax relief.

The articles of incorporation are public documents. Once you get it approved, you can show it to your lead sponsors for getting more donations

In order to cut costs, many NPOs operate virtually while registering in countries with the lowest filing fees. This can cause problems later on.

It is important that your NPO is registered in the district where you are offering major programs or services to receive tax exemption from the IRS there.

What Should Be Included in Articles of Incorporation for Nonprofit?

The articles of incorporation are different for each country and state. Most of them, however, include the same elements mentioned below.

Make sure you include all components step by step according to the guidelines given below:

NAME OF YOUR NONPROFIT ENTITY

The articles of incorporation begin with the name of your nonprofit entity. Choose a name that is not already registered with the state. This is particularly important as the government does not allow two businesses to be registered with the same name.

Also, you must make sure to comply with the following state laws when writing the name of your organization in the article:

Abbreviations Inc. or Corp.

In some states, you are required to add a designator to your organization's name such as Corp. or Inc. For example, if your name is Pet Shelter, you might have to add Pet Shelter Corp. or Pet Shelter Inc.

Some states consider nonprofits as a corporation (Corp.) and do not require you to add the designator with the name. Make sure you know what the law is in your state before adding this part.

Don't Use Words That Suggest an Alliance With Some Specialized Firms

Avoid using words that predict your association with some federal or legal bodies like National, Federal, US, Syndicate,

Trust, Republic, or Cooperative. Also, don't use terms that make you look like a profitable business such as Bank, Doctor, or Lawyer.

NATURE OF YOUR ORGANIZATION

All articles of incorporation include the nature of the business, for example, a nonstock corporation, nonprofit, or a Limited Liability Company (LLC). For an NGO, you mention that your organization is nonprofit with its sole purpose belonging to the public benefit.

The Internal Revenue Service (IRS) will check if your article contains the following three points:

- The nonprofit will only benefit charitable causes
- Earnings will not be used for personal benefit
- Assets of the nonprofit will not be distributed to the owner or the directors upon dissolution

Overall, the IRS wants to see that your NPO is formed for public benefit, not to benefit yourself. You have to mention the exact language provided by IRS in your article while drafting these elements.

Make sure that your supporting documents support the points given above. Mentioning the type and structure of your NPO (such as charity, hospice, healthcare, or pet shelter) will get you a strong base to get the draft accepted, by both secretary of state and IRS.

ADDRESS OF YOUR NONPROFIT PRINCIPLE OFFICE

According to the law in some states, you are required to mention the address of your NPO head office.

You can also use a virtual address for your NPO in case your organization runs globally or you do not wish to maintain a permanent location in one state. However, refrain from using P.O Box as your main address in the article as it goes against the laws of many states.

CONTACT DETAILS OF YOUR REGISTERED AGENT

A registered agent is a person who receives official documents on the behalf of your organization. His/her location is used as a primary address to send or receive tax notices, annual reports, and notice of litigations. The articles of incorporation require you to mention the details of your registered agent such as his/her name and address.

In most cases, the address of the registered agent is different from the main office, but it can be the same in scenarios when the nonprofit officer is acting as the registered agent.

It is important that your registered agent lives in the same state where you are filing your articles of incorporation. If your business operates in another state, you will have to find the agent in the same state as your incorporation. Also, he/she has to be available during office hours to receive and sign documents which makes a virtual address non-suitable for them.

THE DURATION OF YOUR NPO

Some laws of incorporation necessitate mentioning the life of your NPO. Since most organizations don't have a specific expiration date, they prefer mentioning perpetual or perennial.

CONTACT DETAILS OF INCORPORATORS

You will have to mention the names and signatures of all the incorporators in your article.

An incorporate is the undersigned of the charter document who is involved in preparing and registering the article with the government. Depending on your organization, you can have one or more incorporators.

CONTACT DETAILS OF YOUR BOARD OF DIRECTORS

This is a crucial component to make your draft look appealing as the directors are the strategic backbone for an NPO. The board of directors is responsible for making strategic and financial decisions for your organization. Hence, you should make sure that your board members have good communication and fundraising skills with diverse experience in strategic management and handling money.

The articles of incorporation require the names and addresses of the directors (also known as superintendents). The number of directors required for the NPO depends on your state. Also, you can change the names of the directors later by submitting a restated article of incorporation for nonprofits.

PURPOSE STATEMENT

Nonprofit articles of incorporation include a statement of purpose stating the goal of the project. The statement of purpose states why your project deserves a 501c3 tax exemption.

The statement of purpose in your document will use the exact language as mentioned by IRS given below:

"Said corporation is organized exclusively for charitable, religious, educational, and scientific purposes, including, for such purposes, the making of distributions to organizations that qualify as exempt organizations under section 501(c)(3) of the Internal Revenue Code, or the corresponding section of any future federal tax code."

ADDITIONAL MEMBERS (IF ANY)

Many companies have additional stakeholders who take part in the major decision-making. For example trustees, voting members, or any other clubs involved in decision making. However, we suggest you restrict decision-making only to your board members. Adding extra members will only complicate your organizational structure.

OTHER POINTS TO HIGHLIGHT YOUR NONPROFIT STANDING

IRS suggests including the three elements to highlight your organization as NPO. The points should be included separately, with each containing a clear paragraph in the formal language.

It Is a Not-For-Profit Organization

This section will state that your organization will not use any part of the earnings that will be distributed to the members, trustees, or other stakeholders except for the compensation to the employees.

You will also include that the property your organization owns is solely restricted for public benefit and non of its part will be used for business or profit.

Will Not Participate in Any Forbidden Activity

In this element, you will specify that none of your organizational activities will carry propaganda or benefit any particular political campaign. Also, the corporation's activities shall not be dominated by propaganda or any other act aimed at influencing legislation.

The Assets Will Be Distributed According to 501c3 Rules in the Event of Dissolution

Businesses usually start as nonprofit and then distribute assets among themselves upon dissolution. Adding this statement is compulsory as it will show IRS that you comply with the rules on all levels.

The section will highlight that in case of dissolution, you will distribute the assets to the government or federal bodies to be used for public benefit.

AMENDMENTS (REINSTATED ARTICLE OF INCORPORATION)

The articles of incorporation are amended under two following conditions:

- It gets rejected the first time: Your article can get rejected in case it does not comply with the IRS requirements for tax exemption. In such a case, double-check your statement of purpose, nature of your NPO, and supporting documents.
- The organization's structure changes after its approval: You will make amendments in case your organization gets restructured such as changing your registered agent or directors. In such a scenario, the changes will have to be approved by 2/3rd of your board members to include them in the article.

Amending the articles of incorporation is hectic and costly. Therefore, be sure you take the right steps when making your initial decisions and article of incorporation.

Are There Any Other Steps I Need to Take?

Once you are done with your draft, make sure you do the following things to take your organization off the ground.

Check Your State's Website to Check the Article Requirements

As mentioned earlier that every state has its requirements for issuing the certificate of incorporation. For example, some states necessitate you to mention statement of lawful purpose or statement of specific purpose in addition to the "statement of purpose". In such instances, you can find the language, citation, and even templates on the government websites. Also, some states require you to draft your document in a particular font, alignment, and spacing. To ensure that you don't miss any important information, check your state's laws before you write an article. You can also take a professional lawyer's help from your state in this regard.

Do Name Research

The government does not allow two organizations to be registered under the same name. Therefore, double-check the name you have selected for your NPO. Each state has a dedicated page for checking if the business name is already taken. Also, there are several business name generator tools you can use to find a unique name for your business.

Create a By-Law for Board Members

After you draft your articles of incorporation, you will make a by-law statement for your team members. This will act as the guideline for your organization to outline the laws and regulations to be abided by. In some cases, you will have to submit it along with your articles of incorporation.

Bring Your Stakeholders on One Page

Bringing your board members on one page is important both before and after the article of incorporation. They decide what programs will be implemented, what budget will be required, and how funds will be raised.

Most organizations follow the traditional way of board meetings where they meet weekly or monthly for discussion and planning.

Start Your Fundraising

After you get your article of incorporation approved, it is now time to start your fundraising. You can try unique fundraising ideas to collect more money for your projects or do paid marketing campaigns. Don't forget to check the budget for each fundraising campaign to ensure that you don't exceed 15% of your fundraising goal.

WAYS TO RECRUIT VOLUNTEERS FOR YOUR NONPROFIT

Recruiting a strong group of volunteers for your nonprofit is truly a marathon, not a sprint. You find a great volunteer, but then for various reasons, they have to step back. Don't get discouraged, and focus on engaging more people ready to get on board with your mission. Here are 20 fresh and encouraging ideas to help you achieve success in your recruiting efforts.

Healthy Serving Culture - Before you even start to invite new folks into your organization, take time to look (and even ask current volunteers) how things are running and where improvements can be made. Your current volunteers can be some of your best recruiters, inspiring others with their positive experiences.

Become (or find!) A People Person - What if your passion for your nonprofit is off the charts, but your ability to communicate that passion finds you tongue-tied? Let me first suggest that practice makes perfect — get outside your comfort zone and start talking! If you're not quite there, find others in your organization with the gift of gab and ask them to staff your booth at volunteer fairs, ask questions of potential volunteers, and share the vision with potential recruits.

Always be Recruit Ready - Here's the scene: you are hosting an event unrelated to recruitment and someone asks about volunteering. Don't get caught without a way to get their information and follow up! Remember to always have a clear plan to share volunteer opportunities. Create recruitment kits with information about your nonprofit (and maybe a bumper sticker or pencil) and be sure to collect their contact information.

Create an Elevator Speech - Part of being recruit-ready is creating a quick 30-second explanation of the vision and mission of your nonprofit. Teach it to your other staff and volunteers so they can share this mission statement along with their personal experience when they meet those who might want to help.

Be a Joiner - Start investing in community relationships that are already within your organization and look for opportunities to collaborate with other like-minded nonprofits. Those relationships will likely grow more connections. Or, if your nonprofit is new, start joining meetings and conferences with other nonprofits, and ask about best practices for volunteer recruiting. Don't be a loner, be a joiner!

Ask Questions - Kimberly Gatchell, founder of the nonprofit RISE Dance, shared that she doesn't just need dance instructors. It takes a village to run a nonprofit! She asks lots of questions to build relationships with potential volunteers:

- What do you have a passion for?
- What makes you excited to help?
- Do you love social media?

- Do you feel most alive when you are behind the scenes or working with people?

Be Willing to Share - Kimberly went on to say that if after asking these questions, it doesn't seem like a fit, she isn't afraid to recommend other nonprofits. Once you begin to "be a joiner," you will become aware of the bigger nonprofit community's needs. You might find that you start a trend of nonprofits recommending other nonprofits to people looking to serve in different capacities.

Sleuth Your Social Media - If you have social media accounts, look at your comment section and note the people who frequently like or comment on your posts. Don't be afraid to reach out to them individually, thank them for their interest, invite them to an upcoming event, or just ask directly about their interest in hearing more about volunteer opportunities.

Recruitment Business Cards - Consider ordering business cards with your nonprofit's contact information and a brief description that your team can hand out if an interested potential volunteer comes along. Use these as part of your recruitment readiness kit!

Giving Tuesday/National Nonprofit Day - Giving Tuesday (the Tuesday after Thanksgiving) and National Nonprofit Day (August 17th) are two "holidays" which can be utilized to encourage folks not just to give financially, but challenge people to give their time.

Maximize Special Event Opportunities - Make use of a one-time event for your nonprofit (think fun runs, pancake breakfasts and other fundraisers) to reach out to a wide audience and those on the fringe of saying yes to a one-time volunteer opportunity. If you host a volunteer fair, make it fun by including games or challenges between volunteers to grab attention and laughs.

Bring A Friend - Everything's better with a friend (or family member)! Challenge your volunteers to bring along a friend or family member as they serve and offer your nonprofit's bumper sticker or another small gift for their time. Collect their contact information so you can share more about ways to help at future events.

Celebrate and Recruit - Organize a volunteer celebration where current and former volunteers are welcome to bring guests who share their passion for your nonprofit's mission.

Circle Back to Volunteers - It never hurts to keep in touch with past volunteers and reach out again to share new opportunities or positions that are needed. It may be a better season of life to serve and they are ready to again give their time.

Recruiting with a Title - In your recruitment efforts, it may benefit you to give needed positions a more specific title so potential volunteers will be able to match their skills with your needs. For example, if you need a "one-time event logistics coordinator" this could be appealing to those who can only volunteer on a limited basis.

Find the Balance - It's wise to communicate that you immediately need to find volunteers, but also give people the opportunity to say no if it's not a good time or fit. Communicating that balance seems less manipulative and is a healthy way to approach recruiting. Desperation is not effective when it comes to engaging long-term volunteers.

Look for Out-of-the-Box Opportunities to Recruit - Use festivals, conferences, college fairs, women's organizations, church missions-emphasis Sundays, and other community-organized gatherings to promote your nonprofit. The United Way offers a service called "Get Connected" to connect volunteers with nonprofits and may be available in your area. Look for virtual opportunities to connect and recruit.

Be Resilient - Take a no as a "not now" instead of as a "not ever." Don't be afraid to circle back, send invitations to events to keep them interested and stay in contact to see if their schedule might be opening up.

Offer Flexible Opportunities - To encourage recruits that they aren't committing for life, consider offering a set time frame to start with (6 months or a year), after which you can both evaluate the serving experience and make decisions about future volunteering.

Encourage Growth - You may encounter a volunteer who is willing but lacking a necessary skill to really maximize their time with your nonprofit. Don't be afraid to suggest developing needed skills (like counselor training, musical training, or computer skills) before joining you.

Investing in your nonprofit's culture and relationships will work wonders to build your volunteer force. By engaging others in your mission and utilizing some of these ideas, you can grow an amazing team of volunteers.

PAYING EMPLOYEES AS A NONPROFIT ORGANIZATION

Nonprofit organizations must pay their employees or workers enough. The Fair Labor Standards Act ("FLSA") states how employers must pay workers such as minimum wage and overtime pay.

Both for-profit and nonprofit employers must:

- Pay covered workers at least the federal minimum wage or the state minimum wage if higher;
- Pay overtime when covered, non-exempt workers work more than 40 hours in one week; and
- Pay overtime to covered, non-exempt workers at a rate of at least one and one-half times their hourly pay.

What does "covered" mean?

There are two ways that workers are "covered", or protected, by the FLSA:

- If they work for certain organizations ("enterprises") or

- If they are covered by the FLSA.

Most people that work as housekeepers, cooks, and babysitters are covered if their wages reach a certain amount and they work for more than 8 hours per week for one or more employers.

Enterprise coverage

People are protected if they are workers of an enterprise and their nonprofit employer:

- Has annual sales of greater than $500,000
- Does business between states or
- Is a hospital, a place providing medical or nursing care for residents, a school or preschool, or a public agency.

Individual coverage

Even when they do not work for a nonprofit with the above rules, workers can still be protected by the FLSA. The FLSA protects workers who produce or exchange goods across state lines. This can include mailing letters across state lines, making phone calls across state lines, keeping records of interstate transactions, or accepting goods at a food pantry that have crossed state lines.

For example, a worker of a new Chicago nonprofit that does not fundraise outside the state, has revenues of $100,000, and whose position involves discussions within Illinois would not be covered under the FLSA.

If a person is a covered, non-exempt worker they are protected by the FLSA's rules and must be paid overtime for any hours worked over and above 40 hours per week.

When is someone exempt from overtime pay?

Certain workers are exempt and do not get overtime pay. The test to decide whether a worker is exempt has three parts:

- Be paid a salary;
- Be paid at least a $455 a week; and
- Do a certain type of work.

A worker must pass all three parts of the test to be exempt. The salary requirements do not apply to teachers, outside sales workers, and workers practicing medicine or law. The third part of the test (type of work) is the hardest to define.

Type of work defined

A nonprofit organization must classify its workers as either exempt or non-exempt based on the person's type of work. Exemptions are defined under the FLSA. Nonprofit organizations should carefully confirm the definitions prior to classifying workers. The following are some examples of exempt workers:

- Executive. An exempt executive employee's work involves managing the work of 2 or more other workers and hiring, firing, and promoting other workers;
- Administrative. An exempt administrative employee performs office or non-manual work for a nonprofit and makes independent decisions regarding important matters;
- Professional. An exempt professional does work requiring an advanced degree or they do work that requires creativity, invention, or imagination in an artistic job;
- Certain computer workers. The computer employee exemption refers to people with

specialized knowledge of computer systems.

What can happen if a nonprofit organization ignores the FLSA rules?

It is not an option to ignore FLSA rules. A person can file a lawsuit against their employer if they have not been paid properly. For example, workers can sue their employer if their employer:

Lists them as exempt from overtime payment by giving them important job titles but then requires them to perform non-exempt functions;

- Requires them to work "off the clock" and then does not pay them for this work;
- Fails to pay them for the number of hours worked; or
- Fails to pay them the correct overtime rate of at least one and one-half times their regular hourly rate.

A nonprofit organization must take the time to assign work tasks carefully. And it must classify, pay, and keep required records of workers to avoid lawsuits.

How much should a nonprofit pay its employees?

Tax-exempt charitable nonprofits, like all other employers, are required to follow federal and state wage and hour laws that require employers to pay minimum wage. At the upper end, compensation must be "reasonable" and not "excessive," which is a fundamental requirement of maintaining tax-exempt status. It is helpful to know what the going rate is when you are hiring a new staff member by reviewing "comparability data," which are data about salary and benefits from other nonprofits in the same or a similar geographic area, with a similar budget and mission focus. Many state associations of nonprofits collect salary and benefit information via regular surveys, and produce state-specific reports that allow nonprofit employers to compare compensation of similar organizations by job titles/responsibilities. These data may be free or discounted to members as a benefit of membership in a state association of nonprofits. Those state-specific compensation reports can be found here. There are also national compensation surveys available for purchase.

Minimum wage and overtime

Employees must be paid the legally mandated minimum wage, that can differ state-to-state; there is also a federal minimum wage rate. Employers should pay whichever is higher. If employees (not independent contractors - it's important to know the difference!) work more than 40 hours in a work week, be aware that the nonprofit may owe those employees overtime compensation.